Sins & Sunflowers

Emma-Jane Barlow

Second Edition

To Cath

Thank you for your support!

love

EJB

First Published in 2022
Second Edition Published by Lulu Publishing 2023

ISBN: 978-1-3999-5909-4

Edited by Emma-Jane Barlow
Cover art by Emma-Jane Barlow

Printed by Lulu Publishing

Previous books by the author:
Darkness & Light (2020)

Emma Jane Poetry
@emmajanepoetry
www.emmajanebarlow.co.uk

Visit the author's website

"Emma-Jane Barlow weaves a tapestry of emotions and thoughts that leaves a lasting impact. Each line is carefully crafted, revealing an underlying passion that resonates deeply. Sins & Sunflowers: Second Edition invites readers to embark on a journey of introspection and discovery through a unique perspective. Read it!"

— David Scott, BBC Radio Manchester Host & Bestselling Author of Mancunians

"As a self-professed 'poet-witch' Emma-Jane Barlow draws on hard-fought pain and promise, hope and heartbreak to cast a powerful spell. Using language and imagery that is both accessible and complex, readers will be pulled to walk the road to healing with her. Sins and Sunflowers: Second Edition is a testimony to the power of words to rewrite and rewire our story and ultimately, open ourselves to more love than we ever thought possible."

— Kim McKellar, Poet & Visual Artist & Author of What The Earth Already Knows, Is This Not A Holy Place & Go, Wake The Bear

"Emma-Jane has created an extraordinary poetry collection filled with a menagerie of emotions. From disappointment and heartbreak, exploration and growth, to hope and new love, this book celebrates the journey to joyful wholeness. A picture of truth and honesty, 'Sins & Sunflowers: Second Edition' is art we can all relate to, as well as learn from."

— Kimberly McAfee, Poet & Author of AmerAsian

"Full of emotion and with a deep understanding of human frailty, Emma-Jane Barlow guides us through the pain and sorrow of heartbreak, the freedom that comes with letting go and the joy of self-discovery. Emma-Jane's poetry is rich in reflection and soulful imagery. Through each line, we are shown the strength and hope that lies in each of us to overcome adversity. She reminds us that we have the power to heal ourselves. A beautifully written book and cathartic to read. I highly recommend."

— Emily Paget, Poet & Author of The Weight of Missing

"An exhilarating collection of awe-inspiring poems. A feisty, sassy, strong comeback from a bestselling poet, who takes you through her healing journey of transformation, learning to love yourself, finding love and experiencing pain and betrayal. Raw, honest, beautiful poems that capture the heart with gorgeous metaphors and imagery. I have many favourite pieces. Emma-Jane shows us that you can find love again. She shows us that love truly does conquer all."

— Saira Anwar, Poet & Author of The Death of a Beautiful Dream

"Emma-Jane Barlow's 'Sins and Sunflowers: Second Edition' is a captivating testament to the profound transformative power of words. Through her poetry, she intertwines the essence of nature, immersing readers in a world that vividly reflects her deepest emotions as she journeys through different moments and experiences. It is truly beautiful."

— Dhayana Alejandrina, Poet & Author of Agridulce

"Sins and Sunflowers: Second Edition is a rebirth. It is a vulnerable collection of poems displaying perseverance amidst life's trials and tribulations, the way we rise among the chaos. I loved the line 'You can't break a constellation without changing the shape of the galaxy forever.' It's such a gorgeous line and thought. I'll be thinking about that for a while. Emma-Jane Barlow takes her readers on a journey of healing, a process known to many to be achingly beautiful and never-ending, one we learn hope through. This book is for the hopefuls."

— Alexis Mitchell, Poet & Author of I Write, Therefore I Am, Hope Chest & The Attic

"Emma-Jane Barlow takes you on a poetic rollercoaster of emotions with Sins & Sunflowers: Second Edition. It is open and raw. The real-life relationships discussed are relatable. The quality and depth of each written piece is mesmerising. A commendable collection of poems."

— Hafiza Issa, Poet & Multi-Award Winning Author of Earmuffs To The Moon

Dedicated to all of those who have suffered from a broken heart, are on the quest to find new love or embarking on the journey of learning to love yourself.

Introduction

Healing is a continuous journey. When I first started writing for Sins & Sunflowers in 2021, I was still picking up the broken pieces of myself. I was struggling to process the aftershock of dealing with my first heartbreak, which changed my entire existence. Everything I knew to be true was gone in a flash and I had to navigate through it in the best way I know how; to write about it.

As an autistic woman, I find meaning by inking lines of verse. Through poetry, I understand my experiences and how they have shaped me into the person I am today. After the publication was released, I found that I was still writing poems that could go in the book and I felt strongly that some parts of my healing journey hadn't been expressed in the first edition of Sins & Sunflowers.

First of all, nobody tells you how complex the healing process is when you not only lose somebody you once loved but grieve a version of yourself that you will never get back. This has been particularly difficult for me to manage. I had to start again. Figure out who I was and what I wanted my new life to look like.

In a short time, I experienced a whirlwind of changes including new faces, new homes and new love. I've had to face trauma I had buried deep inside myself and find the inner strength to purge people from my story. I've learned that not everyone in life is meant to stay. Lovers can become strangers, friends can become enemies and people who were once your family can become faded memories that only live on in photographs.

I also learned some painstaking truths about myself and the role I played in my own ruination. I've had to accept that I don't have control over everything that happens in my life.

The hardest part of the healing journey for me has been letting go of what could have been and mourning the wasted time I spent being unhappy. There are years of my life that I won't get back and I spent a long time blaming myself for not seeing the truth sooner. For not leaving the first time I found myself afraid of my partner, for not putting my needs first, for not valuing myself enough to find a love that would spark my soul instead of drain it. Time is the greatest gift we have and only now do I truly understand how precious it is.

Loss and love are entwined in the fabric of my mind. I was pulled apart and I had to stitch myself back together again. Even now, I'm still trying to find a new balance and learn to live in the present moment. My biggest fear always has been and always will be, that I will lose the people closest to me. And I still battle with my insecurities and struggle with the intricacies of relationships, but I'm still learning.

In this second edition, I uncover my deepest secrets, in the hope that my vulnerability makes someone who picks up this book feel a little less alone. From the highest highs to the lowest lows, this has been a life-changing journey and I wanted to share more parts of the story with the world.
So that the heartbroken could feel less lonely, the romantics could feel inspired and the happiest people could experience what it's like to truly fall in love all over again by reading my words.

The human experience is complex. I have experienced a spectrum of emotions in the last two years of my life. I have felt it all. From seeking revenge to forgiving those who have harmed me, to reliving every memory, the good and the bad to ultimately finding some closure. It's been a wild ride and I have cried and fallen apart so many times, but I made it.

I'm not saying I am fully healed from my experiences. On some level, I believe we never truly heal completely. We carry our pain with us. But as time passes, we feel its weight a little less each day. And I'm finally at a stage where I no longer let my past define my future.

Heartbreak. Trauma. Betrayal. Gratitude. Lust. Love. These things inexplicably change our hearts forever. I have changed a lot from my experiences but not in the way I expected. I realised, once I was free from a toxic relationship that I had a voice, something to say, something to share. My confidence grew the moment that I realised my worth. It is through the power of poetry and absorbing the strength of the positive people in my life that I grew into this new version of myself today that is writing these honest words.

The labyrinth of life can be hard to navigate. We will never know what awaits us in the future. If there is anything I have learned from my experiences, it is that gratitude is the only true way we can remain in the present moment. It's the only way to not get swept away into the what-ifs. Now, I capture the beauty in my life in every way possible, in photographs, in videos, in music and of course in poetry. I let my art speak because my words are my legacy. Here is the full journey for you to savour. I hope some of it resonates with your soul. Enjoy the second edition of Sins & Sunflowers.

Emma-Jane Barlow

Ink is just ink
a heart is just a heart
and time is just time
everything fades eventually
even the blood-splattered
pigments of your sins on my skin
— this was just the death of us.

But I will decorate
my bones with sunflowers
ignite the decay with hope
find solace in knowing
that I had a lucky escape.
I found the hidden key
it's time to mould
the new shape of me.

- *Inkblot, Emma-Jane Barlow*

Contents

May your heart remain breakable
but never by the same hand twice.
Without your past, you could never have
arrived — so wondrously and brutally,
by design or some violent, exquisite
happenstance — here

— Taylor Swift

Sins & Sunflowers

Second Edition

Weeds

You will find me in the weeds. Anchored to the soil. Solar plexus tied to the earth with invisible ivy, rooted in an arid wasteland where dreams go to die. I close my eyes and wish with all my might that I could be a sunflower with canary wings and float above it all. Choose when to be grounded and when I want to escape. But you will find me in the weeds. Anchored to the soil. A victim of crumbling stone eroded over time, worn like a willow tree creaking in a lonely meadow. I see a shooting star, kiss the earth, pray to the skies for guidance but the Gods are not listening. They want me to figure it out on my own. Scratch crimson scars into my pale innocence and learn the art of healing. But I am tired of living amongst the weeds, of the sadness that spreads like a fungus, consuming me and dimming the flickering amber that still survives, even after the harshest storms. You will find me in the weeds. Anchored to the soil. Swaying into old patterns, lured into the darkness because it feels safe, familiar and inviting. It begins as a whisper, merging into a witch's cackle, then it morphs into a voice like mine until I can no longer tell if something feels like me. It gets loud sometimes, here in the weeds. As others tend to their gardens, pruning primrose and sprinkling seeds, building hedges to hide their true ache with flowers. I am here, amongst the weeds. Alone. Just me and the elements, fighting, growing, shrinking. Endings and new beginnings. I close my eyes and wish with all my might, that I could be a sunflower. But maybe yellow is not my colour? What if my destiny is to claw my way to greatness? I just have to fall and fall and fall, until I am worthy to wear those canary wings.

Dark Ink

The crystalline city of their love lay in ruins
and she made a necklace of icicles —
wore it to thwart any more dark ink
from settling inside her heart like a
pond of sorrow — every tomorrow
brought more ache and lamenting over
the betrayal that almost dismantled her soul.

But her heart is a vacuum for love —
it craves the allure of sparks and
intimacy — affection is her drug
and every kiss and hug nourishes her
inner child and it soothes —
a rose can bloom from concrete walls.

Someday we'll tell fireside stories
about the woman that used a needle
and thread to sew her battle wounds
before she bled — people will gather
and admire the poet witch that drank
her pain like snake venom — used it
to fuel her repentance and find a
balance in the karma she always
knew existed.

If you come looking — you'll find her
drawing hearts on the
pavements with pastel chalk
a dagger behind her back — waiting
for the next man to dictate her worth
and this time — she will be ready
to expel any dark ink from the crystalline
city that she has started to construct
for herself.

time to Shine

And onwards I go, madly spinning —
until I am caught in a distant orbit.
Surrounded by stars that lived
inside my bones for so long,
that I don't recognise them now —
as they glitter like diamond emblems,
radiating a million possibilities
awaiting my grasp — and I cry,
as I see these shiny parts of me
glimmering in the raven sky,
so many facets that I have yet
to discover, freckles that I will
learn to love — memories
that have yet to be drawn
with charcoal wonder,
across the blank pages that I
see before me.

I stretch open my palm
the lines have vanished.
"Try again" whispered the universe.
I wipe away my tears and place
my hand over my throat chakra.
Violet warmth kisses my neck
like a past lover — but this feels different.
This is the strongest type of love.
From the root of my soul,
the marrow in me,
I allow myself
to be truly free.
"Try again" whispered the universe.
The stars don't blink, they don't
want to miss a thing.
"Try again" whispered the universe.

"This is your time to shine."

tightrope

We were walking on a tightrope
for years, eyes closed, periwinkle hearts
barely beating but we didn't notice.
We stayed — suspended, waving
like a white flag and none of us wanted
to surrender to the density of the truth.

That we drifted apart.

We curled our toes like crescent moons
and tried to hold on to the stars to keep
us floating and maybe, if you hadn't strayed
into another galaxy, we would still be there
hovering, too afraid to let go of something
that died long ago.

Nothing Is Ever As It Seems

Nothing is ever as it seems
we try to mould the seconds
of the day like clay — create
potted memories and grow
daisies that shine and dance
in the wind to the beat we made
but — we cannot build everything
with bare hands — we must let go
of the need to carve and sculpt
every memory we wish to hold
we must be bold — let the
universe work its magic.

I know it's hard
to let go of the future you have
so fiercely painted — but it's
time to let it go, darling —
just let it all go and trust that
the love you have lost will be
nothing compared to the love
you will find — for yourself.

The pain will not hinder you forever
the clock will soothe your scars
with the ointment of time
and the space in your chest
will be filled again with starlight
— just hold on and remember that
nothing is ever as it seems.

Dangerous Hope

A little bit of hope is a dangerous thing.
A scintilla of love, a freckle of light
peeping its way through the ether
like coyote eyes glowing red.
But without hope, there is no fuel
to jumpstart my heart.

I plunge into desolate rivers
without a serrated piece of driftwood
to pull me aboard. I reach for the holy stars.
I am yearning for a taste of what we had before
the blackout.

Maybe the stars of our past had to die
for us to see the fresh beauty of life again.
But I will cling to the dangerous hope
for a brighter tomorrow.

And before I go to sleep,
I whisper goodnight
to you into my pillow.
Hoping it travels to you somehow.
Don't give up on us.
Please, let us try and hold on
to what we have built.

You can't break a constellation
without changing the shape of the galaxy forever.

The Fourth Of November

Remember remember the fourth of November.
When the stars in our galaxy exploded,
not in celebration but in sadness.
As the festival of light was born,
we were wrapped in a bandana of darkness
choking on the smoke,
with no oxygen fumes
to save us.

This was the day I was stained red
like a poppy in mourning.

I will always remember the fourth of November.

No amount of scrubbing will wipe me clean.
No amount of bleach will erase this memory.
No amount of new days will stop me
from saying your name before I sleep
even though I know you cannot hear me.

Waves

I have always loved the water
but feared incoming waves.
For so long — I have had you
to help me stay afloat.
But now, I must ride them alone.

Face the typhoon monsters
without the safety of your arms
or the sound of your cradle song.

I must dip beneath the surface,
discover how to swim again
through harlequin coral reefs,
treacherous currents
and avoid poisonous algae
because you were the antidote,
the sails to my boat.

I am blind — gaining my sight.
Moving away from blue and you.
Finding new colours that I can call my own.

Colours In My Hair

I painted colours in my hair and laughed today.
For a moment, I forgot that you were no longer mine.
A semblance of normality, I almost felt fine.
Then the icy river trickled down my spine
as salt startled me with the stark signs — of reality.

I will have to learn to live
with this cavern of sadness
and adapt my mind to this madness.
How can you be my everything and nothing all at once?
Here I am in emotional limbo, wishing away the months.

I am craving your kisses and your vanilla scent.
You were my safety, my anchor, my cement.
Now I am free to fly, but my wings are weak.
I am running out of rhymes and truths to speak.

I just wanted you to know that I still care.
And show you that I painted colours in my hair.

Museum Of My Mind

I sometimes forget that we are no longer together.

Then a flashback pulls me down to my knees —
the bathroom floor feels the collapse of my universe.
I pour sugar into the wound
trying to sweeten the sting, as I —
fall into our memories
drenched in nostalgic longing.

The millions of kisses we shared
noteworthy moments
we carved into this land,
all still in the museum of my mind
behind protected glass.

My tears don't stop
because I know
this wound will never heal.
It will always be there,
a stalker in the shadows,
a thorn in my side,
an unlucky penny
lodged in my throat.

My lungs are rotting.
Rubble stacking like bones
tearing down our kingdom
until there is no space left
to breathe.

I have a colander for a heart
and it won't stop bleeding for you.

Coda

I thought I knew what it felt like
to be broken.
But my soul has perished
with these words we have spoken.
As I s c a t t e r across the floor,
scorch the earth with my pain.
I know we will never be the same again.

It settles in my stomach
like a laden pill.
That we have reached our coda
and I love you still.
Our song has reached its final note
but I'm still drawing treble clefs
with melodies of hope.

I Don't Recognise Her

I don't recognise her.
The evanescent ghost staring back at me.
She has strayed from so many paths,
she no longer sees the winding road
that leads to the place her heart calls home.
The trembling compass is a moment away
from oblivion — black tears staining skin,
bone and soul.

I don't recognise her.
She hides with the monsters under her bed —
as daylight scorches her lifeless eyes.
She is a fractured vase holding weeds
that once shined, they died of thirst,
wilted from hurt, her fingernails
scratching the ruthless dirt.
Seeking reason, praying for salvation.
Besieged by the cruelness of the situation.

I don't recognise her.
She waltzes in the shadows,
but this time, it feels different.
She doesn't know the way.
Her map reversed,
seaweed submersed — in menacing water.
Her reflection is an apparition,
a contorted image of how faith and love
can so easily be shattered
and how it is entirely possible to be a ghost
— even if your pulse is still beating.

Withered Roses

Withered roses always seem prettier to me.

The delicacy of being broken a million ways
allows the aureate beams of authenticity
to shine through and I see it like a beacon.

I am drawn to people who have lived
in a cage with chaos and survived.

The fighters, the fierce and the fallen.

Maybe I have a purpose to not only
heal myself but to stitch a
patchwork quilt with my lessons
to keep others warm?

Maybe I connect with other withered
roses because their shades are similar to mine?

We are no longer a bold shade of vermillion,
but a dusty grey demanding it to rain red
so we can soak up every pigment
to feel

whole again.

Storm Heart

There is a storm in my heart.
And I cry with the rain
to feel something outside
of this striking solitude.
The release from
the clouds pacifies me
into a spider web of
stillness — then grief
swarms in my chest like
a rabble of hungry bees
the howling increases
in the nightly breeze —
I let go of the need
to know where this feeling
goes — my body is trembling
but like the roots of a tree —
no storm can get the best of me.

Red Ink

Behind the veil, I am disguising my truth.
My heart is a jigsaw of jagged pieces,
I am trying to discover the full picture
of me again — but there is a slot missing
just a blank shape with your name on it
scribed in red ink.

I hope it never fades.
I hope it never fades.
I hope it never fades.

Behind the veil, I am disguising my truth.
We loved each other fiercely, blazing, bold,
in this, until we are old.
But now, I scatter crumbling petals
over our gravestone — we are dead yet still alive.

A long chapter has ended,
we each have
a new journey to take,
a new story to write,
trying to understand
what we are to each other now.

But it will never be the same,
nothing will ever be the same,
I wish with all my might that
we could be the same.

Behind the veil, I am disguising my truth.
I am vulnerable without you.
The softness of the pillow
catches my tears like a weeping willow
it billows under the weight of my woe —
why did you have to go?
Even if we tried, we couldn't be us again.
So here I am, captivated by your name,
scribed on me in red ink — it's everywhere
my heart, my skin, my eyes.
I see the remnants of your face
across the starry skies.
I see the pools of blue,
the essence of you.
I am clinging to it all.

Behind the veil, I am disguising my truth.
I am standing on a bridge — in limbo
bear traps surrounding my feet.
There is no right move or place to go.
I can hear your voice — whispering
notes of love and promises.
Inside I am splintering,
the plaster is breaking,
I am disguising my truth from the world
because my soul is breaking.

How Did We End Up Here?

How did we end up here?
I don't recognise you anymore.
Your heart is adorned with barbed wire,
you have pierced it, now you are hissing,
spitting, lashing out because
you love me so deeply
that you are losing your mind,
blindly — reaching for my hand,
but I'm not there, I can't be, not right now.

How did we end up here?
When I look in the mirror, I look away
because I can see inky nebulas
engulfing green, I see so much of you,
every forehead kiss, compliment
of my beauty, even my hair —
I see your hands in it,
brushing it away from my face,
just a memory now — dust in the dungeon
of what was never meant to last.
I still feel your touch — this is all too much.

How did we end up here?
I don't recognise us.
We want to grasp the vines,
find a step to reside — in the home we built.
Find a way to exist in this new reality,
hide in the turret, forget any of this
happened — but we can't.
The ink has stained the paper with blood
and we cannot absorb the same blood twice.

Bleach

You dipped my heart in bleach
— drained it of its cherry essence
and polluted it with fatal fumes
I consumed it — every molecule of me
absorbing the darkness you kept
hidden for so long — I am tripping
on a drug I didn't choose to take —
how could I not see that
you no longer liked the taste of cherries?
I felt your anguish when you told me
you had made a mistake —
but it was just crocodile tears and
a charming joker playing a card trick
with the queen who owned your heart.
You were a red herring but I
didn't see the smoke rising —
I should have looked up at the sky
more — maybe I would have seen
the truth in skywriting or a hidden
message in the clouds — just something
— anything — that could have warned
me about you.

The Match

You lit the match that ended us.
But I didn't moulder into ashes,
I became the whole fucking phoenix rising,
much brighter than you could have imagined.

You lit the match that ended us.
But I didn't wipe my tears with
photographs of you for too long.
I stored them away like a time capsule.
Moths dying without the moonlight.

You lit the match that ended us.
But I didn't embrace the company
of shadows and wine for too long.
I walked into a sober existence,
one without my addiction to you,
one without the weight of my dependency,
one without feral scratches
clawing in the pit of my stomach
that were always there but I
couldn't figure out why.

They should have warned me,
that you were never the hero,
but the villain — a man that unravelled,
became everything he swore
he would never be.

Pick 'N' Mix

Maybe after years of standing
in the pick 'n' mix shop, choosing
the same sweet every time you
decided to try something else?
You hovered over the one with
the familiar taste, sweet and
long-lasting — dependable,
loyal to you — but the tangy
sours catch your eye —
the sprinkled sugar gives
you the illusion that it will
taste like me — but it won't.
Salt and sugar are the
twins of deception.
You scoop them up and make
a choice — the wrong one.
You can't go back now.
Every time you look at
that pick 'n' mix selection
you will know what you did
and what you lost —
I'll be a haunting memory
of glistened tears —
echoes of heartstrings
snapping — the burden of shock.
You will no longer enjoy the
honey of my lips — but I will
explore — find out more and
discover that life can indeed
be sweet again.

Merlot

I know I will not find the answers
at the bottom of this glass of Merlot.
But as the carmine warmth of plum
and blackberry stains my gullet
like a burgundy remedy.
I feel the burning tang of courage
slowly soothing my grief
— putting it to sleep.

Sip by sip.
What you did stings a little less.
Sip by sip.
All the lines become blurry.
Sip by sip.
I don't love you anymore,
a lie I tell myself.
Sip by sip.
What you did stings a little less.

I know I will not find the answers
at the bottom of this glass of Merlot.
But the bottle is giving me comfort
even if it is just for a moment.
So I can feel senseless.
Detached from the hankering
I have for you, cease the nexus
of my heart to yours for a minute,
so I can hear the sound of my own
existence beating.

I put a dark cloak around my
pale delicacy, covering the bruise
you left with powdered strength
so that people think
I am a warrior.

They think I'm the
Goddess of Heartbreak
who slays dragons with
an iron heart but these
chambers are really
made from mercury petals
— they are melting as the wine
becomes a labyrinth of ribbon inside
— I think I might be losing my mind.

And I try
to say goodbye
and I cry
I can't deny
that there is love
buried beneath the disgust.

I scream until the bottle is empty
— I feel empty.

You did this to me.

Worthless

I am worthless
just an explosion
of heart and limbs
and cartilage, sewn together
by loneliness — nothing
can lift this crushing
skyscraper on my
chest — I can
hear the fissures of
my frame cracking,
bending, breaking.
Waking to a nightmare
circling around my head
like a murder of crows.
Black grief blocking
the sunlight and unlocking
my knee joints — so I
shudder and wobble and
fall into the tempting dirt
like a dandelion
without a stem.
Worthless. Hopeless.
Gutless. Darkness.
I can't feel the love
of the sun anymore.
For me, you will always
be winter.

Sacrilege

You will pay for your sins,
just as I will for mine — but my heart
never crossed the line — that you did.
Your love is tainted.
Rancid blood
leaks into my valves.
You are intoxicating
my innocence with your sacrilege,
dirty mistakes and infectious lies.
Will I ever feel clean again?
Pricking my fingers with a needle
squeezing out blood,
shame leaking on the marble
bathroom floor in the shape
of devil horns.

Your transgressions
are staying with me,
long after we separated and
time and time again,
I cannot forget
how many years you chose to lie,
look me in the eye,
carry that burden and
poured it into me
like laced wine,
besmirching my honour
and giving me an ailment
that can never be cured.
I will search for a remedy regardless.

I will not let your sins
become my own.

Catalyst

I was meant to experience this loss.
To accumulate this gaping chasm
inside my soul to learn to mine for
my shade of gold — channel the
light in my life I have been craving
for years — find a major for these
minor black keys — find the pixie dust
that would lift my pneuma from
my body — so I could watch it dance
like a solo firefly in the forest of truth.

I didn't know it at the time.
But I know now this loss was
the catalyst — the pivotal point at which
I would explode like a dormant firework
— filling the heavens with colours
I didn't know I had the power to create.

I was meant to experience the loss of
you — so that I could allow more space
for my roots to flourish — create
a monument of words in the ravines
of this earth — that will withstand the
ravage of time — and I couldn't do that
in the dwelling of your shadow.

Parachute

Do you believe everything happens for a reason?
Because I do — I know deep in the quintessence
of my being that this brittle heart of mine
was always meant to rupture.
I am destined for a life of
aching and breaking,
ripping and rebuilding,
clawing and falling,
I just never thought it would be you
that would cut the parachute strings
— you didn't even try to save me.

You gave up on us, long before
I found out about your loose lips.
Your wandering eyes found new flesh to devour.
I waited at home in our bed, awake with the moon,
not settling until I felt the heat
of your body next to mine — so, no, I'm not fine.
I don't believe I ever will be.
These scars are rooted in the core of me.

But I have to trust the universe.
Believe that there is a reason for
this chaos — to shake my spirit and gift
me a new pair of eyes that will only
see through a lens of self-love.
I know that someone out there
will love me in ways you never could
but first — I must pour every drop of
violet hope into my veins,
give myself the wings I need to fly solo
because my parachute days are finally over.

Enormity

I don't understand the enormity of this heartbreak — my brain is shielding me with its cushioned walls — the trauma of your kisses are becoming sinister echoes when the sun goes down — everything is fading yet still so bold — I'm drinking a potent liquor with an aftertaste of you — I am trying to forget — but I know that you will always live in the crevices of my being — be the crumbs down the side of the sofa — hidden away but your presence is known — silent but a collision of organ keys making melodies every time I wake to greet a new day — songbirds waiting in the trees — I don't understand how to deal with this — the lair that you carved with your selfish spoon has left me gutless — I have to plant the kernels of my intuition again and learn to trust myself and my choices — I was so sure of you — for years you were the vowels to my consonants — the apple to my oak tree attachment — the vines to my crumbling walls — the enormity of this scares me — but over time you will wane like a hand-drawn heart on a condensed window — the footprints in the snow will be swept away by the growling wind — I will change and evolve in a way that you never expected — the enormity of this still scares me — but I can feel the pulses of my comfort zone leaving my chassis like purging a witch's spell — I'm making space for new branches to grow — my confidence sprouting like a colourful mushroom unearthed from hiding in the barren ground — I know the hands of the clock may have to travel the circumference of a year or more until I can eliminate you enough to not feel this burden — but loving and hating you at the same time has become my normal existence — I could laser the ink like a repentant tattoo but it wouldn't abolish the sorrow or the truth — the vivid ghost that is you — I don't understand the enormity of this heartbreak — but I am trying and that is all I can expect from a maimed soul — who is learning to love herself and discover what she is truly worth.

Lonely Raindrop

There is an ache in my bones tonight
as I listen to the rain
ricochet off the windows
and I think about what it must be
to live as a lonely raindrop
dripping down a window
racing to the bottom
full of vigour and moxie
not knowing that its path
is going to end.

And I know how it feels
to be blissfully ignorant
of what lies ahead.

I know how it feels
to be fooled by the
waxing moon and be
blinded by its beauty.

We are all raindrops
creating trails
trying to leave a mark
but this lonely raindrop
has stopped moving
because of a broken heart.

Foundation Of Betrayal

I'm doing it again
unravelling
tight knots
coming undone
the mayhem of my mind
is stumbling into
the doors of the past
unpicking nails from
the wood until my
fingers bleed
and the pain resurfaces
I am dancing to
the pulse of what-ifs
and trying to change
the memories of you
that are embossed
in my brain like a
bold tattoo
I am trying to build
a home with warrior walls
unshakable pillars
that can withstand
future hurricanes
but no matter
how hard
I try or cry
the foundation of betrayal
still remains.

Alone

Being strong doesn't mean that
I don't crumble like a sandcastle
in the dark — it is when the moonlight
glisters, that the ache of it all engulfs
every pore of me — I shiver like a leaf
in the winter wind because when the
sun sleeps and the warmth fades —
my mask cascades, revealing the
naked truth of my pain, it is messy,
all of this, cracking, breaking,
splintering but also embalming,
healing and soothing for my soul,
to know how it feels to be alone.

Devil In the Sea

When I look into your eyes,
I see the devil in the sea,
he's been there all along,
cloaked in waves and
shimmering with so much
blue — that I got lost in you,
believed that I was your world,
the most beautiful girl,
our love was to the moon and
back, remember?

But maybe we never made it
beyond the Earth's atmosphere.
What if the last twelve years have
been an illusion, a warped reality
that I created with the blind brushes
of my imagination?

Did you think of me when you sinned?
How it would break my skin like walnuts.
Leave me open to falling grenades
and make me bleed every dream I
had for you and me, watch the past swirl
down the plughole and mourn a future
that would never be.

All because you couldn't hold
me and tell me the truth:

That I was no longer enough for you.

Debris

After Nikita Gill

There is nothing beautiful
about the wreckage of a human being
the dynamite and detonation
of fossilised stitches
ripping at the seams
the horrific hauntings of limbs
flayed and floating in the ocean
that swallows souls.

Freckles of war memories
bobbing on the waves of pensive
longing like gnarled wood polluting
any beauty the sunrise reflects
to reveal a blink of hope.

Healing is an exquisite journey
of finding room in the cavities of
your existence to hide away
your trail of debris.

But from everything broken
there is always the birth of
a beautiful mosaic.

I Don't Need Anyone to Love Me

I don't need anyone to love me
is the biggest lie I tell myself.
I hear the foreign syllables leaving
a taste of petrol on my tongue,
and I know that one trace of
amber will kindle my self-deceit
and I will collapse like a straw hut —
caving inwards and revealing
the vulnerability I try so hard to disguise.

I don't need anyone to love me
is the biggest lie I tell myself.
I look at the black discs swelling
in my teal eyes and I can fool
others but not hoax my reflection.
It is there for me to see — brass
and bold — the fear of being alone.
It grows like a seedling, suffocating
every inch of me until I grasp on
any leaf or nearby tree for stability,
pining for the roots that he poisoned.

I don't need anyone to love me
is the biggest lie I tell myself.
I watch from above, as this new
version of me clutches onto
anything and anyone to find the
tenderness that has vanished,
replace the dying rose petals
with virgin life, beauty that
can sparkle in my eyes and
heart once more.

I don't need anyone to love me
is the biggest lie I tell myself.
As I look at the chalk outline
of a missing man in my bed,
my teardrops confirm that
our love story is dead —
I am on the journey towards
forgiving you, so I can let
you go, so the next body
that lies next to me will
never leave like you did.

This Pain Is Mine

This pain is mine — only I know how it radiates through my body like a magma wave — painting me with shame when I remember what he did — only I know how the cavernous ache grows behind my navel — swirling into a cyclone of longing as I crave for his touch that I know I will never feel again — only I know how the pain has changed me — a rooted scar in my nucleus — being pulled by tweezers every minute of every day until I bleed out — but no one can see the stains in this white dress embellished with feminine strength — no one can see the tears I carry in a bottle in a chain around my neck marked with his initials — a violet and indigo bruise decorates the space where my heart resides — but you see a thriving heart pouncing — feasting its fangs into someone new to love — I'm just a wounded animal — craving a syrup I have absorbed from an IV for years — I'm addicted to the safety of wholehearted love but now I must learn to love alone — get my fix from the shape I see in the mirror — only I know how the pain mocks me — just when I feel the urge to laugh or smile — the pulsing starts like a wisdom tooth wanting to be removed — but I can never erase the splinters of him — no fuel or matches will destroy how entrenched our love goes — this pain is mine — not yours or even his — don't fit my pain on a scale you designed for your comfort — it cannot be made small — folded like a pocket square neatly presented to make you feel good and useful no — this is my pain and only I will choose how to feel it — I will not leave it beneath a trap door so that you can see the glimmer of my teeth — I will not hide it in the shadows so you can see me "getting on with it" — healing is unequivocally messy — and this is me giving you plenty of warning — like a church bell announcing an impending storm to the villagers — that this is the beginning of my pain — so many whirlwind days and earthquake nights are approaching — my armoured skin will emerge with new cracks and I will not cover them up with the concealer society wants me to use — this pain is mine — it is valid — it is unpredictable — it is my reality — so please — don't pretend you feel its weight.

Sieve

I can't sleep tonight.
And I don't know if it is
the raindrops knocking on my window
or the past knocking on my heart,
asking politely to come in,
but if I let it, I know, with a gust of wind,
it will be overtaken by the lifeblood of you.

I have already drained my heart this week,
used a sieve to filter out the shards of glass
that were still piercing me, even now,
when a picture of you arrives on my phone screen
like an amber alert, urging me to remember
the stubbornness of this pain that you left me with.

Why is it so hard to heal?
I grow new skin but then it stops,
melts away until I am raw,
exposed as a carcass in the desert sun.
I have to begin again.
One step forward and three steps back.
Grains of salt falling through a sieve,
I never really stood a chance.
I will always be broken now
— and it's all your fault.

But this isn't my first mosaic
you are just a flint in my soul,
eventually, the pain will leave,
I will become the sun
and no longer give you the power
to enter the sacred gates of my mind.

Fountain Of Rage

I did it.
I deleted your number.
But I didn't delete you from my mind.
Your voice is like a scratched vinyl
whispering to me when my head
nestles into my pillow each night.
Your presence plagues me and I don't
want your ghostly kiss to leave an echo
on my forehead any longer.
I don't want to remember your radiance
or the way you looked so deeply
into my eyes, it was like we were
the only two people in existence.
No, I can't miss you like I want to.
There is a fountain of rage bubbling
over the misery and I wish it would
simmer softly and evaporate
but I believe it will take more time,
more reason and rhyme before
I am ready to let you go completely.

Landmine

The truth is.

I was afraid of you.

Our love was built on a landmine.
And I still remember the first time I lit the
fuse — my peach skin bruised
by your sharp tongue and heavy hands
you made me question my
worth — this was the birth
of my voice dwindling — I was too young
to know how to fight back — so I kept our secret.
Every volcanic eruption and lovers corruption
was sealed behind a closed door.

I made you angry — so many times I saw
your irises glow a devil's red and when they
cooled — returned to blue — I pushed down
my shame and I forgave you.

I thought this was love. I didn't know any different.
I was just mimicking what I saw in my parents
as a child. I thought relationships were meant
to be loud and wild. Unpredictable and unshakable.

But fear was the foundation of the cherry tree
we planted — a dozen years of sweet and sour
moments and now — when I look back.
I only taste the unsweetened version of the truth.

You needed help but now I need it too.
As I sit in my therapist's office, the walls are closing in
when I realise everything that happened between us

was not okay.

Whale Song

Some memories echo like a whale song
vibrating bones and finding a home in
the marrow of your mind — a melody
so deeply rooted in your being that with
every reflection in the mirror you see it
change you — you coil like a spring
as you watch the way it wrinkles
your skin like a map folded
multiple times — it has faded
at the corners and morphed into
a rusty shade of anguish you thought
time had forgotten — but it's still there
— as bold as amber — branding
your heart — letters of love — symbols
of betrayal and loss. They are there
and they are never leaving — no matter
how many times the moon duels
with the sun.

Sacred Prayer

You were my sacred prayer.
I would whisper your name into the cosmos,
reverberating my love as a tender melody
into the night sky and you would always answer.

I can still feel it now.
The vibrations of our souls aligned in perfect harmony.
The universe smiled, as we walked with our hands
and hearts locked like steel chains.

But I was in bed with a trickster all along.
There was no meant-to-be.
Now I am on my knees worshipping
an altar of stars that shine just for me.

The voice that once guided our love
is giving me the strength to live a life of free expression,
to dance without a partner, to create my own rhythm
for the first time, this slow dance is mine.

I whisper into the cosmos once again,
but the only voice I hear is my own.
The past version of me smiles as glitter rain falls
like star diamonds and dazzles the
sleeping power in my heart.

"I'm proud of you." She beams.
"This is just the beginning."
"Your prayers will be answered soon."

Sparks

Sparks in December
as the frost falls
and my fractured heart
is still dipped in crimson
from the scars he left.
But tonight — I carve away
a tiny piece of my heart,
leave it out in the open,
for you to decorate with
new shades of glitter.

I feel your pulse next to mine
as you hold my hand
in the dusty dark.
Stroking my finger —
electricity jolts to all the
places that have been in
hibernation for so long
— and I know you feel it too.

You laugh — and the sleeping
wings flitter inside my chest
— I never dreamed they would
attempt a flight so soon.
Kissing in your car, I truly
felt alive, wanted, desired.

And in that moment —
I knew it was possible
to be heartbroken and happy,
to miss him but want you,
to lose the idea of us
but find myself,
to know everything and
nothing all at once.

I am embracing the sparks
in all their golden glory
— and if they die,
I will search this island
for a new beginning,
find the warmth and glow
in another's embrace.

I am letting my heart endure
so much more in its fragile state
because I know its crenels are unshakable.
I am unlocking the door,
turning the key — giving my heart
the space to be free.

And Just Like That

And just like that.
The moon became a witness,
to the birth of something new.
As the snow began to thaw
inside my soul, festive warmth
trickled through the gaps like
warm cider — reaching the farthest
corners, attempting to wake
the idle magic that
refused to shine
after he broke me.
But you let me trust
for a brief moment,
in the joy of tinsel
and intoxicating fire.
Tentative footprints on
echoing cobblestones,
loud enough to believe it
was real and not a clip from
a movie scene.
I know there will be icicles,
embedded in my arteries
like snake fangs for some time
and I am anything but fine
but — for those few days,
everything flowed like opulent wine,
fawn bedsheets and kisses aglow,
and just like that,
I started — ever so slightly
to let my inhibitions go.

December Mist

Under the moonlight, beneath the December mist.
Log fires and laughter, another wine-stained kiss.
A black and white village, sparks in streetlamp glow.
Anything can happen, there is little that I know.
About the man holding my hand to keep it warm.
Butterflies burst from hibernation.
Are you the calm after the storm?
Anticipation and longing hang like opal wishes in the sky.
You try to mend my broken heart with that
twinkle in your eye.
Giving me a reason to believe in jubilation.
To see hope in decadent fragments
and the beauty of celebration.
Twinkling Christmas wreaths and icy droplets shine.
This moment and future memory
will only be yours and mine.
A polaroid snapshot of taking time to discover.
Each other's souls and goals,
getting to know one another.
Under the moonlight, beneath the December mist.
Twisted in lustful linen, another wine-stained kiss.
Black and white village fading,
streetlamp glow shining brightly.
Morning birdsong tapping on your window politely.
Naked heat and fervour kissing me sweetly.
Losing my need for control, embracing you completely.

Isn't It Exciting?

Isn't it exciting?
That the road ahead
has melted into an asphalt river
for you to swim to a new island
you created with your bare hands?

Isn't it exciting?
That the invisible cage has rusted
the lock and you can stretch
your jaded wings for the first
time in a vestal sky?

Isn't it exciting?
That you can now devour
every crumb of ecstasy
you didn't know you were hungry for?

Isn't it exciting?
To know that you are birthing
a constellation — forming a
dot-to-dot existence that belongs
to only you and no one else
can claim it?

Yes, it's pretty fucking exciting.

Shapes Of White

Take me to a cabin in the woods
where I could get to know you
by the firelight glow — blankets
and raw flesh — windows
decorated with snow.

Melodies of the forest and
howling winter song —
sensual notes would rise
— it wouldn't take too long
for the saffron flames in our eyes
to kindle — we'd watch the
snowflakes mellow
the sinless daylight dwindle.

The blood moon bespeaking our
heart's most hidden desire —
lips find their way to skin
losing sheets of covered attire.

Shapes of white inside the cabin
twisting and tongues dancing —
whispers and wildness,
racing and romancing.

Take me to a cabin in the woods
and jumpstart my mangled soul —
kiss me beneath the weighted white
and fill my body with coal.

Heat the ice he left and
let it melt away — take me to a cabin
— my inner vixen wants to play.

Ink Blot

I thought of you today.
You drifted into my mind like
an empty cloud and I did not let
it rain — I did not let myself feel
any pain — no — I just accepted
that you were a ghost with a
visitor's pass — an inkblot on
blank paper — expanding
until you dried — making a
shape of nothingness.

I could squint my eyes with all
my might but not see anything
at all — it's only deception that
my brain wants me to see —
maybe it's protecting me?
Sheltering me from the
razor shards that you left
the clock must spin and spin
until my heart pushes out
the glass naturally.

I will erase every trace —
the salty taste of betrayal
on my tongue will sweeten
and my tear ducts will lose
the memory of you.

The inkblot will never become
anything at all — I will stop trying
to generate a reason for
all of this and see that:

Ink is just ink
a heart is just a heart
and time is just time
everything fades eventually
even the blood-splattered
pigments of your sins on my skin
— this was just the death of us.

But I will decorate
my bones with sunflowers
ignite the decay with hope
find solace in knowing
that I had a lucky escape.
I found the hidden key
it's time to mould
the new shape of me.

Rhythm Beneath the Mirrorball

I'm not afraid anymore
of embracing the chaos — twirling
beneath the mirrorball,
eyes closed — just me and the beat,
only I know the rhythm of my feet.
There is no direction — or answers
waiting in my reflection.
I am a spirit without chains,
rain, just let me dance in the rain!
Squeezing my toes in the sand of life,
learning to love the dirt,
caress the hurt, glass fragments
becoming earrings for me to wear —
there is no burden I cannot bear.
The weight of the world on my bones
may cause them to fracture,
but I am a warrior with a sunshine
rapture — this golden orb inside my heart,
the one that births this beautiful art,
it has the unlimited strength of Athena,
I have the soul of a poet,
the grace of a ballerina —
but when the mightiest storms arrive,
I know how to survive.
When the mirrorball falls,
I am waiting for it all —
ready for the tambourine
that will shake my peace,
the melody changes
and so does the beat.

One Day I Will Stop Loving You

One day I will stop loving you.
But not tonight.
This time and space is reserved
for me to rue what we could
have been and I am locking onto
the memories with tiger claws.
Dragging my thoughts back into
a jungle of what-ifs and abandoned dreams.
Draping a curtain of fiction
over the true words of our
not-so-happy ending.

One day I will stop loving you.
But not tonight.
This time and space is mine
for me to submerge into
perilous waters and hold
my breath, lamenting the
death of the man I thought
you were.

One day I will stop loving you.
I am praying to the universe to give me
a sign, a symbol — something
to tell me that I will be okay without you.

Our Spot

I sat in our spot today.
The bench where we met.
It's winter again, just like it
was all those years ago.
Tree bones and despair.
The last remnants
of Autumn trodden on
the ground beneath people's feet.

The irony of the cenotaph
that stands bold in the centre of
this place is the remembrance.
I look at the blood-red poppies
on wreaths but all I can think
about is the war that we had,
the battle cries we sounded
as we sunk into our demise.

There is a bird's nest in
one of the trees and for me,
it signals new life.
I am in a new life now.
One without you.

The joy of February snowflakes
has been replaced with January
hope and abiding self-love.

This is no longer a spot that is ours.
The Arctic Sea flows through me
as my memories and feelings
coalesce.

It isn't the bite of winter,
but the teeth, fierce fangs
that you left behind
that are gnawing at me
to never move on,
even though you already have.

But one day soon,
I will walk by our spot.
My heart will be as numb
as blue lips, and I will hum
the songs we used to sing
through an unfeigned smile.

Any day now...
Any day now...
Any day now...

Secret Agent

I feel like a secret agent.
Skulking in the shadows.
Scrolling and watching
you fall in love
with another girl.
I am a hawk with a
heavy heart with
talons that unfurl.

I wish for karma to
strike and for the
sweet milk to turn.
Your relationship is
blooming and I want
to watch it burn.

I can almost hear the
echoes as you both laugh
at my impressionable heart.
I thought you were just friends
but you were deceitful from the start.
And when he cut the strings
and he was finally free.
I bet you couldn't wait to
steal him from me.

So I watched from a
distance and let it all unfold.
The flames danced
until the trail went cold.
He broke her heart too
and I knew it wouldn't last.
So I buried them both
with headstones
in the graveyard of my past.

Poetry Keeps Me Warm

I am the city that never sleeps.
This vessel wakes to scribe
soul runes throughout the night
on blank walls to ease the ache.
Poetry keeps me warm.
When the chill of existence
seeps into my bones —
like tar coating every inch of me
in sticky and unfathomable
loneliness — poetry is there.
A candle burning in
the iris of desolation.
The sugar sweetening the
black coffee of uncertainty.
Poetry keeps me warm.
Even when icicles fall.
Poetry saves me.
Feeding me sunlight
on a spoon.
So I can stay alive
just one moment longer.

Forgive Me

Forgive me, for I have sinned.
Took one too many sips from the devil's ambrosia
to dull the pulsating rhythms of your treachery,
reaching out into the dancefloor of deceit
with blind eyes to crash into a stranger's lips,
tracing the lines of right and wrong to find
the sugar you stole from my sweetened soul.

Drawing a broken heart on an etch a sketch,
erasing it over and over again, seeking
a way through the fog of desperation to escape
the trail of anguish that now follows me.

Forgive me, for I have sinned too.
The blue in you has left a steel dagger in my daisy heart
and the consequence of the hurt has made me feral,
wolves gather around me now, to see who can
take a bite of me, sensing my vulnerability, hunters
charged with virility.

So forgive me, as I obliterate everything I know to
rebuild and uncover the rest of my love story
without its usual narrator.

Forgive me, as I toy with the idea
of sharing another's bed.
To feel the softness of a man I barely know,
to keep hold of the rope that burns.
I'm like the desert without the heat.
I'm shivering in this avalanche and I see
an inferno in this glass — as I tipple and ripple
into a wave of calamity.

A Woman Undone

I am a woman undone.
Unravelling like a vermillion
ribbon kept in the drawer
for a special occasion.
Sprawling out across the floor,
waiting for my desires to be met.
Craving bare flesh to cure my loneliness.
Alabaster skin waiting for fingertips
pulsing across my landscape
like a piano, playing the right notes.

Reach the places that I find pleasing.
Give me the climax after the action.
Throw me like a ragdoll to remind me
that my bones are not made of glass,
that my warrior strength can take
a little rollicking with you
and my heart
can leave its cage for a while
to be kindled on hot coals.

Maybe all I want is sweaty and sticky
in-the-moment love?
A captured scene instead of the
whole reel of film.
Baby, be the spirit to my cocktail,
let us be shaken and stirred,
create a naughty memory or two
that will gift us the heat
to get us through
the coldest winter nights.

Fuck the Patriarchy

Fuck the patriarchy — I can hear the critical whispers as I cut chunks of my heart out with a knife and fork — leaving it on different plates to see who has the potential to love me more — women are given the illusion of freedom but when they are free — people line up to clip their wings so effortlessly — they pigeon-hole them with commitment and moral ideals — but I say stop the judgement and let me discover — the melodies of what I look for in a lover — playing sharps and flats until I find the middle C — finding out what is right for me — why must we be tied like wedding bands — hand in hand — so everyone can understand our choices?

Fuck the patriarchy — we have all the choices that we do — you would think the fluidity would flow but some statements stick like glue — like the word — slut — rut — constantly stuck in this misogynistic way of thinking — drinking the nectar of female inferiority — the majority of people accept that women can indeed have it all — but some wish for us to fall — find a place on the ground — to not speak so loud and proud about what we want — what we desire — fire me up and I will not be silenced — I am a woman who will do what the hell I want — I am brave and bold — a startling savant — no archaic chains will hold me down — I am capable of polishing my own crown.

Fuck the patriarchy — I know this phase of my life should be fun — so stop judging me for this path of destruction I've begun — a woman scorned is a dangerous kind — primed and wise yet hurt and undefined — let me pour gasoline and make my own mistakes — catch the venom from multiple snakes — bottle it and let it fuel me to be strong — find out my definition of right and wrong — so I want to kiss a few frogs in this hurricane of heartbreak? Is that so bad? To feel the golden glow of excitement — experiences I've never had.

Fuck the patriarchy — when are we going to change the way we perceive what women can do and what they can achieve? We need to stop judging them on their patterns of dating — making them feel wrong for their journey of recreating — women are like butterflies — always evolving — solving this problem is so simple — stop clipping their colourful wings — allow them to paint the skies with their love — be enough in the eyes of society — soar and be so much more than the opinions you have of them.

Fuck the patriarchy — there are no limits to female rage — we are channelling the ancestors that fought to give us this space — watch us as we take up this space in any way we can — battling the war started by man — a confident woman is a dangerous kind — I am a woman that knows her mind — maybe I want to be a predator instead of the prey — dating is a game that I want to play — so stop deducing me to a scarlet doxy — I don't need someone to speak for me or be my proxy — I have lips and a heart and a working brain — watch out for my bluntness — as I name and shame — anyone who hurts me or tries to dim my flame — I will savour every grain of sugar from this bitter and harsh culture — where women are the carcasses and we are victims of the vulture.

Fuck the patriarchy — enough is enough — release me from these cuffs — invisible but weighted on my soul for so long — but now I am singing a different song — no more backing vocals — enjoy my solo — capture this moment with a snapshot photo — because this will be the beginning of a woman with tenacity — who does not believe in limits to her capacity.

Fuck the patriarchy and its suffocating restraints — this life is my canvas and I own the paints — the colours of me will bleed through the page — I will take my place — on every stage — talk about my rage and let my words fly — crows from the cage — I am a woman that cannot be silenced — so don't even waste your breath and try — long after I am gone — I hope my words never die — this is what it is to be a woman and what a woman should be — an unstoppable force of nature — lightning in a raging sea.

Fuck the patriarchy — to all the women in the world — don't take any shit — be your boldest self — we are not classic books to be admired on the shelf — remove the dust of your insecurities and take your rightful spot — show the world your strength and shine and give it all you've got — for we were not meant to be muted — judged — used or excluded — we were born to fight — for what is right — ignite and be the flare — ladies we are the jewels of this earth — so always be aware — of the power you own — share your story — use your voice and know that you're not alone.

Snakeskin

My snakeskin heart is shedding.
Layer after layer, peeling away
like chipped paint, until I am raw
and open for new love to blossom.
Some layers stick when I don't
receive the closure I seek.
No full stops in the form of
goodbye kisses or parenthesis
to explain what went wrong.
Just ghostly wonder and waiting
for a reason to surface.

I am blindly reaching out for an
eraser to remove the chalk memories
that are still as rich as bronze
in my mind but in time — they too
will unfurl and decay from the
barricades that I built after the war
with the one whom I named 'forever.'
But now he is a vulgar oath I keep close
to my chest to fuel me to find better.

I am not afraid to fall again.
To gift my soul as a necklace
for another person to wear.
I am brimming with hope beneath
this tough rind, my softness
remains, despite it all.
I am a dove with plasticine wings,
flexible and free, to meader like a cloud
and let love find me.

Phantom

Did I dream you up?
Create you from the
eyelash wishes of my
tattered eyes and conjure
you like a phantom that
would love me, even if
it was only for the night.

Did I imagine the heat of
your body next to mine
as I gave myself to you?
Let you use my body
like a treasure map,
mark every part of my skin
with an X, I can still feel
the sweetness of your kisses.
Did they not mean anything?

How could I have been so wrong?
Trusting another man with my purity
— I am just grateful that I didn't
give you my everything.

There might be an element of
its anatomy missing, but my
heart can regenerate
and I know, after this day of tears
is over, that I will forget your name.

The memories of the weekends
we shared by log fires will turn
into dust, just like the ones
I shared with him — the one that
started this trail of corpses,
the one that instigated this
chain reaction of tragedy.

He was the domino that triggered
this path, his secrets burrowed in me
like a bullet, forever wounded.

And you, phantom, well you
are just caught in the crossfire
of this crazy trajectory of mine,
a speck of story in the vast sky
and you don't deserve
another word inked to this page.

Previous Chapter

Some people stay in your heart
but not in your life — they find a
hidden spot in your atrium
deep in the valleys of your anatomy
— they mould into a shaped memory
and slot into place like bone.
You never forget them
— even when you want to.
Past lovers, old friends,
strangers in the street.
Some are wispy clouds that
float by like a boat on a river —
but some people stay in your heart
and occasionally they whisper
— remind you that
you are a story.
Characters come and go.
Some build doors and some
escape through windows.
Some find a home in your
brain like a campfire and
others fade into the wallpaper
with age — almost like they
never existed or they only
existed in a previous chapter
that never gets read again.

Rainbow Spirit

A rainbow spirit cannot thrive without rain.
Beauty cannot find you in a drought.
You must wash away your
sins and sadness to create fertile land
for sunflowers to sprout.
Do not dig into the valleys of dirt
to find the pot of gold.
For it already exists within you.
Behind the veil of insecurity lies
a gemstone, exquisite and old,
answering only to you.
If you hush and listen, you will
absorb its limitless power and when
you do – you will be a rainbow so bold,
that even the sun and stars will hide
behind the clouds – and you will
outshine them all.

Sext Or Swipe

To sext or not to sext — that is the question I ask myself as my inbox overflows with requests — this is the first time I've been single — so I am trying my best — to experience this new world of modern dating — of swiping and liking — fishing and baiting — wondering if you can be attracted by colourful pixels on a screen — decoding the amount of kisses and what their messages mean — sext or swipe — sext or swipe — searching for a connection — to mend this broken heart and heal the weight of his rejection — discovering what qualities I like in a man and what I can live without — what will be a swipe left without a doubt — the minefield of dating apps is not for the fainthearted — I keep my heart hidden in my ribcage — my trust is shattered and I am guarded — but something starts to happen as the conversations start to flow — it unlocked a different side of me and little did I know — that I could be naughty as well as nice — so I'll explore the kind of woman I want to be — now the chains are gone — it's time for fun and I am finally free.

Shade Of Hope

Hope is the most beautiful
shade of human existence.
It can be found in the petals of
blossom floating in a tenebrous river.
The spark of colour in a monochrome
painting — reminding humanity that
we have a grip on the brush
and it is up to us — to squeeze rainbows
from faded pigments and remnants
of our mosaic mistakes, filament failures
threading through our cores — hope
is the shade of sunrise that pours over
the melancholy blue like saffron candle wax
— gratitude setting in and cooling over
the scars we thought would never heal.

Delicate Lion

I am a delicate lion,
an oxymoron
of rose-petal grace
and alluring courage.
I will pounce and bite
with my feminine wiles,
sink my teeth into
every chunk of flesh
that has the taste I crave
and kiss it softly with
honey-blossom purity.

The gossamer heartstrings
I carry are stronger
then they appear.
The curve of my hips
are ready for the touch
of silk lips, the dip
in my spine
is arched and waiting
for wild memories
wrapped in cotton sheets.

I am spirited and delicate,
an unfurling lotus with a
mercurial curiosity
for impulsive moments
untangling limbs in the
imbued glow
of the watching moon,
roaring as I reach
the peak of pleasure.

Different Light

My heart had to be punctured
to let a different type of light in.
The ravines in my ventricles
are expanding and creating
tunnels for me to explore
the new paths decorated
with pumpkin lanterns of hope.
Sprinkled with seeds
to plant new sycamore trees
to give me shade when I
need to rest a while from
the dizzying chaos of this
new life I am living.
This different light has
the warmth of ginger
and can spread like
a peacock's feathers
inside my skeleton
until I am morphing
into a new form
of someone I never
thought I could be.

The Leaves Are Always Changing

I understand that the leaves have to change but I would do anything to feel the tenderness of your smile every morning, drink the cosmos in the tea that you made for me and feel your soft touch once again, as you stroke my cheek and tell me you love me to the moon and back. But I am sitting on a crescent moon, dangling my feet off the edge, afraid of my loneliness and you are back on Earth, trying not to look at the sky.

I understand the leaves have to change but I would move Heaven and Earth with trembling hands to push back the clock and do something differently. Maybe if we had noticed the fire had burned out we could have filled our pockets with coal, instead of letting our love melt like snow, without you doing something so bold.

I understand the leaves have to change but the cadence of your voice is trapped in my soul locket like a melody of grief. I carry it like a noose and it tightens whenever I am reminded of something in the world that we once shared. Our story is growing mould inside the treasure chest I crafted from the age of seventeen. Lost time comes in waves now and your vibrancy fades like a coffee stain.

The leaves are always changing. I didn't know you would become a memory that would only visit from time to time in the aching prisms of my mind. I wish I knew when it was the last time. I would have held your gaze for a few more seconds and lingered in that kiss instead of turning over on my pillow to sleep.

If I knew what was coming, I would have gripped tightly with cramping fingers to every waking moment. And when I am falling or spiralling like Alice and my soul is running dry or when I am about to cry, I remember the soft touches and the intimacy you and I shared for so many years, I'll never forget what we had for as long as I live and breathe.

Outgrow

After Emily Dickinson

We outgrow love like other things.
Become tired of the ilk —
the texture of familiar silk on
naked bones — we fear the cargo
of the dark and lone —
but crave the esse of extraordinary promises.

We outgrow each other like other things.
The cardigan that no longer has
use — an appendix teetering on
the edge — a loose wire igniting
a shockwave that leads to
a crestfallen reality — Oh!
These ripples of hurt are
stifling — closed eyes and
hushed wishes — dying to go
back to a place where the tide
was safely sleeping.

Anti-Climax

I wasn't ready for the anti-climax.
The kiss without a kick.
I wanted lust stirring
like thunder on my lips.
I was craving the drug
of potential love
expecting a psychedelic trip.

You could have been my lust potion
given me the sip —
to see me floating above
the clouds like a gospel chord
sounding in heart corridors
a praise the lord — moment.

But I wasn't ready
for the anti-climax that I got.

I'm not searching
for beige — I want
burning red flames
magnets in paradise
and postcard memories
taped to the bedpost.

When my lips touched yours
although it was nice —
it didn't wake
the sleeping minx who
wants to play but thank you
for a lovely day.

Happiness Is Found

Sometimes, happiness is found
when you lose everything.
The universe has a way of
cracking open hearts like
fortune cookies to see what
lies beneath the comfort of
needing and knowing.

Sometimes, happiness is found
when you are broken.
Golden vines growing
deep beneath the earth
and emerging from the fissures
climbing up towards the sky
to kiss the sunlight when the timing
is right and the planets align.

Sometimes, happiness is found
when you let go.
Dropping pennies into the ocean
and letting them sink.
Watching pain melt away like
effervescent sugar hearts
in clear water.
Watching the wind carry away
every tumbling leaf of the past
and embracing the wonder of not
knowing what is coming next.

Anti-Valentines

I want to collect every origami paper heart
from every shop window,
place it in a blender
until it turns to mulch,
then drink it like a love potion.
To give myself the affection I give
so freely to others.

I'm not anti-Valentines
but I don't believe one day should
be marked to show you care.
To shout your truest desires
with rooftop banners
and blimps with eternal promises.

Real love is hidden
in the smaller moments
that go unnoticed:
sprinkled like a chocolate
flake crumbled in your
morning cup of tea,
in the sweaty affection
of holding hands
during the same movie
that feels like home.

The space between you
filled with toe touches
at bedtime and forehead
kisses in the dark,
sometimes you don't
always notice the spark
of these ordinary trinkets
of fleeting time and yet,
they are there for the taking,
pearls in our eyes
that we are too blind to see.

Real love cannot be seen
on a greeting card
or in the wrinkles of a
dying red rose.
No, real love is a feeling
and no words can fathom
its inconspicuous glow
you just know
it's there.

The Surface Of Me

I haven't scratched the surface of me and what I can do — there are infant flames in my veins — developing into a blaze that will thrive — when I stop being so afraid to be alive — if I grab a lucky penny and abrade the silver peelings of my past — a window of gold — shimmering like a surprise — a worthy prize to have — a future with no limitations — nothing is stopping me now from conjuring a diamond rainfall to hypnotise me — when I need to be reminded of my inner shine — this world is all mine — to spin whichever way that pleases me — no one said that this would be easy — but if I keep digging beneath the decade mountain — I will find soil that hasn't been touched by my light.

Daisy Chain

Dedicated to the amazing, strong and beautiful women in my life.

I am part of a daisy chain of women.
I grasp my palms with theirs.
Absorbing their celestial strength
on days when my petals wilt with woe.
They are divine blessings with
listening ears, open hearts,
smiles with wings — that reach me
no matter where they are in the world.

I am part of a daisy chain of women.
I learn from their infinite wisdom.
Draw water from their spring when
my heart is parched.
I am in a drought and I crave
a thirst for warmth and love.
Their presence is a weighted blanket
swaddling me from blizzards and
storms — lilac sunbeams radiating
through the invisible cracks of my
fragile windows.

I am part of a daisy chain of women.
I watch as they thrive, survive and fly.
Clipped wings are torn by the
sheer power of female solidarity.
Each soul is intricately woven with
mine — we create a chain of resilience,
soar above the oppression together,
to decorate the sky with our names —
so the world remembers that we were here.

Chemical Reaction

Here with you is a chemical reaction.
A manifestation of the law of attraction.
I feel alive in this morsel of time.
Guitar strings hum with the evening chime.
Moments echoed from movie scenes.
Like a polaroid picture in faded jeans.
Hand on my thigh, the red wine flows,
my heart blossoms, a sinless rose.
Our eyes glint with passion
we feel a divine connection.
Two rivers flow in the same direction.
The curve of your lips invites me in.
It doesn't matter where our destinies have been.
Right now the effusion of intimacy is free.
A blush smoke that only we can see.
The touch of your skin grazing mine.
Our ivory, velvet fingers entwined.
Nothing matters beyond this halo of light.
That glows around us both tonight.
The clock can freeze, the world can wait.
And we can remain here forever on this first date.

Firefly In A Jar

Your laughter rattles through my bones like sunlight —
painting melancholy stains yellow with
your pure and giving spirit.
I can almost see the peeled wallpaper growing
new life, finding its way back to the wall —
different than before — but better — neater, cleaner,
aligned perfectly with my edges — unlike the mess
that was left when he was gone.
Your crooked smile gives my lungs the space
to breathe again — deep and gold — as it always should be,
blessed to be alive — lucky to be in your presence.
The universe sent you to pour joy into my cavities
of sorrow — to remind me that change is good
and there is always someone new you can love —
always a new moment to catch like a firefly
in a jar — shake it until the light guides the way
and I will be brave enough to let my crevices
grow wildflowers from this hurt — to feel the
nurturing essence of faith and believe that falling
doesn't have to be the end.

Beautiful Monsters

It's a hard pill to swallow that I may never be the same again. The beautiful monsters in my mind are in suspended animation, they are a loaded gun, triggered by snowflakes and the saddest soundtracks. They feed off my insecurities, the tasty crumbs left behind by those who have harmed me, those who sunk their teeth into my innocence and took a piece of me with them.

Healing will create new layers of skin but the damage glows like neon paint and only when I try to sleep, do the monsters show themselves in a montage of maudlin memories. Only when the clock strikes midnight do I remember every sorrow in waves, only when the moon peels back its armour to shine do I suddenly feel the density of my solitude.

I see flashes of the devil, the masked man, the wolf and I squeeze my eyes tight. I try to summon happiness in my heart and I think of my shining knight. I remind myself that some time has elapsed, these beautiful monsters give more to me now than they have taken away.

I contort their control over me and carve them into words, picking away at the pieces of my past to produce poetry that provokes.

I sculpt the pain out with a spoon and serve it to the souls who need to relate to it and with every word, I kill the spirits of those beautiful monsters and one day, one day, I hope I find the mightiest sword to silence them once and for all.

Volcano

There is a volcano inside of me
waiting to erupt — my bedrock
trembles at your touch —
my inhibitions crumble to ash
when your kisses get deeper
— keep me on a hook
and tease me — please me
as you whisper the ways
we would play — how you
would heat the magma
in my veins — explain to me
how you would trace your fingers
across my craters until it
is too late and my lava
flows — you know what you
want to do to me and I
can see the visions in your
eyes like flickering fire.
I don't know how long I
can stay dormant —
fantasise about the
ash clouds that would rise
as passion swells in
our eyes — we crave the
same moment — we are
trying to hold back but
it is inevitable — we know
what is coming.

Beautiful Surprise

Darling, you are a beautiful surprise,
I can feel the electricity flowing
from your aura to mine, lips shaped like my name,
begging to be locked with mine.

You are unexpected, a gust of something I needed
when I thought my heart couldn't take it.
Melting me with those soulful eyes,
everything new, magnetised.
Charged with the potential of new love,
whilst picking up the shattered pieces of a love
I have left behind.

My knees wobbled when you kissed me.
Your sunbeam energy shook the foundation
I crafted to protect my feeble heart.
I let go and sink into you like
a battleship beneath the waves.
I crave you and want to know
more, more, explore and feel alive...
Erase the blue and forget what he did
to me and focus on you.

Lust, flowing, a velvet river.
Satin sheets and silent whispers,
I can't bring myself to stop.
But I do and I look at you,
this beautiful surprise in front of me.
When I say goodnight, I am overwhelmed,
in a good way, a kaleidoscope of yellow petals
emanate from blue, I am giving you a slither
of my heart, but please, pretty please,
don't break it like he did.

Echo Of Desire

The echo of desire reverberates between my thighs, hypnotised by the elixir of your eyes, surprised as we go for a ride, slide into a place we can hide, under the sheets, weak knees and our bodies meet, greet me with your hard intention, a coiled spring with burning tension, let go and move into me, see what waves of ecstasy we can create, pupils dilate and the clock strikes eight, keep kissing me until it leads to ten, have me on my back, time and time again, panting until my chest is rising, the tremor of your moans are enticing, say my name until my hands are shaking, earthquakes and handcuffs, memories making. The echo of desire reverberates between my thighs, I have renounced all control when the lust tide rises. I growl and bare my feminine teeth underneath your vigorous posture. I am lost in you, as we power through and burrow down to reach the peak. Chest to chest. Lips on lips. Cheek to cheek. Spicy breath and daredevil tongues, explore. More, more, give me more. The hunger grows between my thighs. We lock and load with stretching sighs. The echo of desire settles into satisfaction. The attraction to you is a moth entranced by a flame. You kiss my forehead delicately and in your eyes, I see my name.

Flamingo Smoke

I don't have a name for what we were because my heart has been tied into an infinity knot — blood clots — in my brain — memories of you will never be the same — your name and your smile are distorted — my ambition to remove you completely is thwarted — but with each passing day — I sway — into a land where the trees we planted wither — the stormy seas are shrinking into a river — the drops of our story evaporating — growing small — falling into the arms of another has saved me from quenching my thirst — from falling for a witch's curse — lost in the romanticised image of the man you used to be —I am rising like flamingo smoke and this is the new me — the past may follow in a trail of deceit — but I have sunflowers growing beneath my feet — I have love in my heart from a worthy man that shines — I am his new religion and he is mine — so stop entering my brain because you no longer belong — songs of sorrow still chime in my soul — but like winter pine trees you have grown old in the cold — so please let me enjoy this summer and soothing light — stay out of the dreams that wake me at night — I am pushing you out and locking the door — I know my worth now and I deserve more — than you — I'm no longer entranced by blue — I am a yellow star blazing with bliss — carving new memories with my darling — kiss by kiss — I don't miss the way you rooted me to the concrete floor — I don't feel stuck or afraid anymore — I don't have a name for what we were because I no longer know what's true — your lies have tainted every sweet memory of you — so I will leave the love story I thought we had in the grave — wave away every rose petal that has turned to dust — I am running into new tulip fields wrapped in the warmth of my lover's lust — dazzled by the love we have started to share — the beauty of me glows through my magenta hair — I whisper softly into my pillow at dusk — smooth ivory wishes like an elephant's tusk — I pray that one day the trauma of him will fade — and I will live my life freely in a sunshine parade.

November Arrives Again

Today, today the fourth of November
it arrives again like rocket fuel
and the stars in a new galaxy
have exploded in celebration and love.
Me and my darling
are a festival of light born
from the bandana of darkness
I was forced into one year ago.
I was choking on the smoke
that emerged from the devil's sea
and he was the oxygen
that saved me.

I was stained red like a poppy in mourning
but now I shimmer like a golden firework.

Maybe I will always remember the fourth of November.

But now I am clean.

Bleach has erased memories of blue –
and these 365 new days have healed
the horrors I had to push through.
I no longer say a name before I sleep
or let ghosts have any power over me.

Instead, I whisper sweet gratitude to the sky
and thank the higher power
for this new love, this new beginning
and this new version of me
that dares to chase comets
into new worlds and beliefs.

She fiercely protects her dynamite now
and only gives it to those who are worthy.

Do You Remember Me?

Do you remember me?
I was the one who called you forever.
The one who believed that the sweetheart
vows we took at seventeen still meant
something about us together.
The one who held you up when your
shoulders crumbled with the weight.
The one who wasn't afraid to stay up late
and wait for your side of the bed to be warm.

Do you remember me?
The one who was your guidance and crutch,
the person to catch you if it all became too much.
The one who was loyal to a fault
and didn't deserve your abuse.
The one who would stand in your corner
and make every excuse.

Do you remember me?
The one who even after knowing your heart
had explored someone new,
would still do just about anything to keep you.
The one who foolishly wanted
to stay in your life, while you stood
with your back to the battlefield,
holding a knife.

Do you remember me?
The one who lost all of her self-respect
on the bathroom floor,
as I begged for a second chance
and I still wanted more.

The one who heard you say
"let's still be friends"
as you offered me a hand.
The one who was too naive to
know and didn't understand,
that what you really wanted
was to have her and keep me
trailing along, you were clinging
to the hope that I would continue
our song and I almost did.

But I was also the one who
was finding love within myself
and learning my worth and potential.
The one who was calming my own storm
and leaving behind the torrential
rain and pain and I knew I would never
be the same, but I tried and I cried
and I fought for what I deserved.

And now I have it.
The love of a worthy man,
and the belief I can be
anything I want to be.

So I ask you one more time.

Do you remember me?

Or am I no longer a worthy memory?
Have you erased it all?
Have I become small
like a deflated balloon in your mind?
Because if you have.
I want to know the secret.

I still remember.
I remember it all.
I remember it all too well.

So well in fact that the movie plays
on a reel and I try so hard not to feel
anything, but I am a leech for the
memories of the bruised and broken,
I remember every fight,
every November night,
every word spoken.

And when I am pulled into the flashbacks,
I fight against the urge to stay.
I blink and remind myself
that you are no longer blue, you're grey.
The colour of ashes and death and decay.

I remind myself that I'm safe now, you're gone.
The best thing you ever did was leave me be,
so I was open to finding a love
that was deserving of me.

The Art Of Loving Me

I am learning to embrace everything.
Neon lights, big dreams and prisms of pink.
The days of not feeling good enough
are starting to sink
to the bottom of the
ocean like relics with toxic traces.
I am ready to explore new places.
Shine as intended and find the perfect hue
to leave heartprints of love with everything I do.
My cramped wings are expanding as my
butterfly soul breaks free.
I radiate until the world shakes,
this is the art of loving me.
Each day, I get one foot closer to
the archway of my fate.
Confetti and sequins embedded
into each moment I create.
Listening to the lullabies
the universe sings effortlessly.
Between the caesura of notes
are the messages meant for me.
I am learning to embrace everything,
I'm not afraid to feel it all.
Butterflies lose their wings sometimes
but I know I would survive the fall.
This is the art of loving me
and I know now what I need.
From now on, I'm a wilful sunflower
I'm no longer a weed.

Moments

Moments that I live for. Crescent moon nights and the breath of summer mornings. Plaid shirt memories and barefoot dancing in the kitchen glow of forecasted love. The innocence of my nephew's smile, as the delicacy of cherry blossom swims around my feet to greet the spring. The choral essence of applause when I recite words on a stage, my heart wings fluttering behind my ribcage like a honey bee drunk on nectar. The saccharine taste of hot tea touching my lips after a long day, kissing the inside of my gullet with simple magic. Moments that I live for. The soaring flight of freedom as a flock of fledglings create melodies across the sky. They do it just for me, at the cusp of twilight as I walk home after another day draws to a close. The benevolence of a friend's words when I need them most. Tears wiped away by the daisy petals of another warrior. Friendship is a fire that keeps me warm when icicles strike. Moments that I live for. The blending hues of a sunrise that fill the sky with promise after a breaking heart starts to mend again. The twinkle of the moon's eyes as she lets me know that everything will be okay. The universe has a plan for me and it is unfolding like an origami rose. I can smell the fragrance and I am finally ready for it.

Moments that I live for. The bold laughter of the man that is allowing me to fall deep into his arms and affection. His laughter refracts from the walls like rainbow faith and my cobalt existence is fading like a ghost. The colours of my life are vivid once more. Moments that I live for. The soothing lullabies of raindrops as they bless my window and I nestle into the valleys of a peaceful sleep, where the yellow waves will take me to a place beyond the shore. Moments that I live for. The cadence of my favourite songs, tapping my fingers and toes to the beat, a hummingbird who has found her voice again and life is sounding sweet. Moments that I live for. The essence of my childhood lifts me like a ruby feather as the rubber swing holds my adult weight. And I remember what it feels like to truly fly, palms up trying to touch the sky, changing the way I feel about the colour blue. These are the moments that I live for. The ones that overwhelm, dazzle and capture this poet's heart. One precious second at a time, I am healing from this metamorphic pain. This wayfarer, with stars in her eyes, is falling in love with life again.

Her Voice Is A Chorus

She kept her voice in a jar for years
and like a bonsai tree — she was
underwatered and afraid — the fragility
of her leaves trembled like grenades
whenever she spoke too loudly
— she thought the walls would
Crumble: soften at the sound
of the sonar she shined behind
her ribs like nuclear waste: the
outstanding magnitude of her
dreams were wearing away like leather.

She watched as time became moss
and snow covered her branches
as clouds littered the
Sky — why did she choose a
mediocre life for so long? Why
did she silence the yellow dove
that wanted so desperately
to be loved? How did she not
see the volcano mist blinding
the white sun? She did not know
a different path until the ivy cleared.

But now — as trauma bonds
uncoil like an ampersand snake
— she recovers from every mistake
and the leaves have grown
iron veins — even when it
Rains: the voice travels
— Soars like an alicorn's
majestic wings and even the trolls
beneath betrayal bridges
can hear the brave song chime
and know what she has become
since that fateful winter.

They were never worthy of her.
Any of them.
And I think they knew it.

She was searching for a
golden watering can and
an elixir so sweet that
it would bless her broken
leaves — and she found it.

Once she had a taste —
She found a new addiction
and wrapped her purity
in a new religion.
He became the stained
glass window in her
monochrome mind
and she would find
salvation at last —

She knows now that
Her voice is a chorus
— one that you should
always remember
— and so she hums it every day
to remind the world

She's here.

Serendipity

You are my serendipity.
An unexpected twinkle in my inky night.
A zenith rose emerging amongst my thorns.
When my heart was thrown
from a skyscraper window,
I had to sculpt wings from the debris
and rebuild a stronger exterior.
The world had begun to harden me.
Then you, with your olive eyes
and endearing smile, you stopped the ice
from preserving my bitterness.
I met you and I felt my heart melt
like a crimson crayon, the colour
seeping into my ivory wasteland
and giving breath back to my tired lungs.
You are my serendipity.
And I thank every star for their orient,
for they gave me you, placed your
name next to mine, in the briefest
moments of time and gave me the
vision for this rhyme.

the Cadence Of A Mermaid Song

I was once the girl beneath the sea — suffocating — submerged by the worst flood in my living memory — limbs dense and dying — decorated in algae — and for all the years I remained still — barely breathing — a stone monument eroding away like enamel on teeth — I was exposed — waiting for my mind to consume me — waiting for my heart to shrivel into a raisin — waiting for my eyes to dim from shiny pennies to obsidian discs with no way for the light to filter through — I was once the girl beneath the sea — the girl who survived on traces of oxygen — and now I am the woman with her feet on land — absorbing water from the roots of Mother Earth's gift and drinking the tonic of gratitude every day — the sun wakes from its brief slumber — I am the woman who climbs apple trees to reach the top — savouring every bite — licking my lips at the taste of joy that lives within my blood — I am hope — I am the peak of a mountain — I am the strength of the moon — I am a vessel where seeds can grow — I am the woman with a heart that expands like summer every time I receive a kiss from my lover — I dance in my dreams again — twirling as an autumn leaf to the cadence of a mermaid song and all along — I realised they did not live in the deceptive shadows of the deep — they were not enticed by the romanticised rock bottom — hidden away from the rest of the world — no — they lay on rocks — sunbathing and appreciating every little beam of beauty that this world has to offer — mermaids are not the devils in disguise — sinking their fangs into sailors and dragging them into the caves of the forgotten — no — they are beings that have seen the murky depths and felt the gaze of the sun and they chose light — I choose light — I choose me — I choose to be free.

I Remember the Sky

I remember the sky when we met.
How it twinkled like the cosmos
in my wild cherry tea, the water
swirled in circles and revealed to me,
that you were the one the tarot cards
predicted, I looked into your forest eyes
and knew right then that I was addicted.

You became my new religion
and I fell hard and fast.
A rollercoaster ride of new love
as I still processed the past.
I remember the sky when we met.
I looked above as we stood
beneath the lampost light.
And saw so much beauty born
on that February night.
Ten hours of talking, kissing and
holding your hand.
A first date that went better than
anything we could have planned.

I remember the sky when we met.
Poetry under the stars and
as the evening rain fell.
The moon winked to let me know
that I was under your spell.
The stars danced in a rhythm
that I hadn't seen before.
That day the corridor in my soul
opened a door.
For him, only for him, he had a
way of silencing my pain.
I had known him in a previous life,
something I can't quite explain.

Just a shiver down my spine
and goosebumps on my skin.
We kissed for the first time
and the connection made my heart spin.

Hello again my love, a voice
whispered inside my mind.
The ink from the sky dropped
on the invisible pages below
as the constellations aligned.

It was a brand new chapter
in my story and he would be by my side.
Even after just one night
I could feel the motion of the ocean tide.

I remember the sky when we met.
Something special was occurring.
The sky giants that were sleeping
were now softly stirring.
Pacing their way across the
landscape of space to draw
our initials in golden ink.
Never in my life before has
everything felt so in sync.

I thought I knew what love was
but until that day with him.
I had been paddling in shallow waters
and now I've truly learned to swim.
I remember the sky when we met.
I won't ever let go of that day.
You captured me and made me
fall in love and you helped me
find my way.

two Faces

Some people have two faces.
A forked tongue that hisses
like the dying ghosts of war.
They wait for you to trust them.
Before striking at the dawn of the blood moon.
They feast their fangs on your vulnerability
and strike when they are close enough to
taste the sugar on your skin.

Some people have two agendas.
First to befriend you
then end you like a full stop. midway
through a sentence.

Sometimes I see a flicker of red in a person's eyes,
but they always manage to disguise their
plan of deceit. I blatantly ignore every little clue
and I did the same with each of you.

Friendship skulls grow dusty in the cabinet of my past.
I trust too quickly and that's why they never last.
I unravel myself like yarn and let you into my heart.
And I know I should be weary at the start
of anything new.

But I never learn.

Nice girls always finish last.
And when I look back at my past.
I've been blindly walking into the masquerade ball,
without concealing my soul's identity.
I need to stop ignoring my gut feeling
and learn to recognise a person's true colours
before they wear my skin like a fur coat
and create a narrative that isn't true.

侘寂 *Wabisabi*

There is beauty in imperfection — how a
sunflower submerged in the concrete loneliness
rises — shimmering its yellow magic
in the wind — blossom falling — becoming
mulch beneath dense feet — the way the air
evolves from ice to heat — the way time
can heal — the spectrum humans can feel —

— everything is temporary.

The cycles we see in nature are a reflection
of what we should see in ourselves — change
is ineludible — you can see it as a monster
lurking beneath the bed — or instead —
you can embrace the fact that nothing
stays the same — there is a wildness
in letting go — surrendering to the
unknown — allowing the universe
to whisper the right direction to you
— spin the compass and trust the guide —
the earth will ground you — the earth will provide.

There is beauty in imperfection — and I am learning
to love my mistakes — accept every fall from grace —
forgive every godless face that has come and
gone from my story.

I'm learning to see the flaws as flowers.
Undeniable buds of beauty sprouting from the soil of
everything that has ever made me ache like winter.

I am living my life by the three principles of Wabisabi:
nothing lasts, nothing is ever finished and nothing is perfect.
So I am going to exist and enjoy my imperfectly perfect life.

The Intimacy Of Being Seen By You

The intimacy of being seen by you is in the way you listen intently to every word I say/even if sometimes I'm not making any sense/it's how you understand that some days I need some space/you know that sometimes my family and friends come first/you know my love language/how many sugars I like in my tea/you give me tight hugs because you know it's my safety/ you give me forehead kisses and tell me that you are proud of me/you cover my ears when sirens are approaching because you know it causes me pain/you hold the umbrella over me more than yourself in the rain/you dance with me in the kitchen because you know I like to live my life like a Taylor Swift music video/you give me your jacket on date night when I feel cold/you leave me the last biscuit/you know my favourite foods/you send me songs you think I might like so I can put them in our playlist/you squeeze my hand when we ride in the back of a taxi/you introduce me to new things/you cuddle me from behind when I am cooking/you always ask me if I'm okay/when I'm crying you hold me and give me time to process when I can't identify how I'm feeling/you see beauty in me/even if I haven't showered in days and my face is bare/you pay for every taxi I get on my own at night/you understand my triggers/you don't raise your voice because you know I lived a life of fear before your love/you see my potential/you respect my boundaries and ask me what I need/you wash the dishes every time I cook/you patiently wait for me to text you to let you know I'm home safe/you talk about our future and smile/you send me long texts because I'm on your mind/you plan adventures and activities that we will both enjoy/you never force me to do anything I'm not comfortable with/you send me spontaneous messages to brighten up my day/you look at me with those hazel eyes and my worries fade away/you make me feel seen/safe/respected/loved/and I know how lucky I am to have found a gem of a man who shows me what I truly deserve/and I never take for granted the little things you do to show your love for me.

Letters Of A love Journey

Dear C
My first crush. I was too scared to tell you how cute I thought you were. But you were the only boy that wanted to play skipping games with me on the playground. I laughed at your jokes until I saw another girl kissing your cheek. I pretended to be sick to miss school that week. I was the girl who wrote poems and didn't speak. But you liked confident girls and I was still finding my voice.

Dear S
I still remember when the teacher paired us up in Science class. I told you it was the Bunsen burner turning my cheeks crimson, but it wasn't. I would create a map of what could be using the freckles on your face. In the back of my Maths book, you held a significant place. I scribbled your initials in glitter gel pen with mine. I slipped a love note into your backpack and I knew I'd crossed the line. I took it out and ripped it into a thousand pieces. You would never know how much I wanted you to see me.

Dear R
My first Valentine. I still remember the width of my smile when you gave me paper roses and a teddy bear before Spanish class. Everyone at school was jealous of me that day. You made me feel special in every way. Our first date was a double date with another couple in school. We went to the arcade and watched a film I can't recall. I waited for you to kiss me, but the day never came. After that, you decided we should just be friends.

Dear A
Our friends tried to set us up together. I still remember them all shouting at me to kiss you. You had a kind smile. But I didn't like you like that. You whispered in my ear that you thought I was pretty. But I knew I had to let you down gently. You asked me out a few more times. But I always said no. You gave up trying and started dating a girl in the year above.

Dear B,
The first boy I ever kissed. But I'm not sure I enjoyed it. A bench in the rain, as people passed by. Your eyes were a pastel shade of sky. You let me wear your hoodie on the bus ride home. You were the first boy to call me beautiful. But the love haze faded when I found out you were flirting with my friend. You called her beautiful too. I texted you that it was over. But I'm not sure it really even started.

Dear M,
My heart already belonged to someone else. But every time I saw you, I thought about what it would be like to run my hands through your hair. I didn't know if you were aware. That I would watch your lips when you talked to me. Wondering if they would feel as soft as they looked. At the end of each shift, it was always you and me in the warehouse alone. I had the chance to cheat, but I didn't. My heart will always remain loyal to the one who carries it.

Dear D,
You are so many chapters of my story. I thought you were mine forever. From our teens to our twenties, we grew together. Travelled through the valleys of wounds and wildflowers. You were the last person I thought would hurt me. But you broke something in me that can never be fixed. You inspired the majority of the content of this book and yet the only word I can fathom is *bittersweet.*

Dear R,
I was under the influence. Cocktails and freedom were a dangerous combination and I knew I could have whatever I wanted. I made my move towards you, the masked man who felt like an escape. We kissed in the club and your tongue tasted like melon-flavoured vape. It took me a few days to remove your number from my phone. But it was nice to be yours, even if it was only for the night.

Dear A
I knew you were trouble. Wolf eyes and December skies. You treated me like a golden prize. Your magnetic force pulled me in and I convinced myself that you would be different. But I guess age doesn't always mean wisdom. As my feelings ran deeper, yours ran cold. Behind your fancy suits and fast car, I saw you for what you were, a coward. And just like that, you became a ghost. I allowed myself one day to cry over you and then I moved on.

Dear O,
You were infatuated with me. We talked for months about philosophy and movies and I couldn't wait for us to meet. You were tall and geeky, shy and sweet. On our first date, you asked for permission to hold my hand. We walked around the museum. But to me, you felt guarded, like you were hiding the truest parts of yourself. We kissed at the bus stop but the sparks didn't fly. But I was willing to try. An hour later, you sent me a novel-sized text. You told me you were not ready to date anyone. You did the classic "it's not you but me" that I read so much about.

Dear E,
There was something about you that was intoxicating. Your humour and the playful way you said my name. It was with you that I truly learned the flirting game. We never met in person but I sometimes wonder what would have happened if I had chosen you. I guess you were the one that got away. Maybe in a different life, we added more pages to the story. But I know that if I had chosen you, we would have been a crash-and-burn type of fling. And I guess my heart was yearning for the real thing.

Dear J,
You are the current caretaker of my heart. And oh my are you the one. The one that makes my heart wings flutter. The one who is my best friend. The one who had me falling in love the day we met. The one who gives the best hugs. The one who gives the greatest pep talks. The one who dances around the kitchen with me. The one who makes me belly laugh. The one who believes in me. The one who feels like a religion. The one who is helping me to heal. The one who blessed me with a new beginning. The one whom I now share a home with. The one I want to write more chapters with. The one who has the purest spirit. He trusts me with his heart and I trust him with mine. I've written all the letters now but you my one, my darling, my love. I put all my faith in the universe. And all I wish for is that your love letter will be my final one.

The Growth Of Healing

You know you are healing when your fears fall like cosmic dust over the necklace he gave you, now sprinkled with rust.

You know you are healing when self-love has restored the calcium in your bones. Your mind was filled with paper aeroplanes flying into different zones. But now you only have one small space reserved for your pain. And you only revisit it during the occasional midnight rain.

You know you are healing when you no longer feel unworthy and in the mirror you see. A warrior with a patchwork heart believing in what new love can be.

You know you are healing when the moon in your soul no longer aches. And you don't replay the mixtape of your mistakes.

You know you are healing when you go weeks or months and you forget. How much hurt you have and how heavy it can get.

You know you are healing when you can see beyond the trees. And watch the rose petals of hope dance a rhythm in the breeze.

You know you are healing when you feel the universe had it right. To rip apart and deconstruct your reality, it's your destiny to fight.

You know you are healing when everything softens and is still. And you accept that the past hurts and maybe it always will. But the spikes of the thorns have worn away over time. You are now at the peak of an overwhelming climb. You can touch the celestial promise in the sky.

And you know you'll be okay now that in your own way, you have said goodbye.

Trails Of Lavender

When I look at you, I see all that can be.
All the dreams I have for my life
and ones I haven't even thought of yet.
Here we are, in our first home together.
We dance across the wooden floors
with the grace of a feather.
We are building a castle of dreams.
Decorating white walls with lilac memories.

When I look at you, I see all that can be.
We bury the seeds of our love into the soil
and watch an infant apple tree bloom
with the sweetness of us.
We are evergrowing.
Soft and sterling: shimmering
like a lucky penny on a pebbled street.

When I look at you, I see all that can be.
I see white lace and sunflower bouquets.
Trails of lavender leading me down
an aisle of adventures that will illuminate
my soul like rainbow lilies in spring.

When I look at you, I see all that can be.
I go to sleep each night and you are
the last thing I think about.
When I wake up, your sunshine smile
is how I start my day.

When I look at you, I see possibility.
And every vintage scar
I have collected along the way is fading.
My heart is no longer a shrinking violet.
It absorbs every honeydew drop of
your affection and I want to spend the
rest of my life beneath your amber glow.

The Time Of Her Death

She bites down on me savagely, anchoring her
teeth into my soul for one more breath.
But this is where the past ends.
This is the time of her death.
Her essence has faded like a caterpillar's eyelashes.
The desolate look in her eyes disappears in flashes.

I saw her in the mirror and I felt her in the dark.
But as I grew stronger, she started to lose her spark.
It's time to unlock her jaw and let her fall into the abyss.
Let her vanish like the ache of a goodbye kiss.

I have moved away from the revenge that tasted sweet.
Drank the blood of my heart before it dried like concrete.
The rose petals that lived beneath my tongue
have rotted away slowly and the journey was long.

She bites down on me savagely
and she pleads with me to stay.
But this brave new potion tastes
like freedom, so I'll let her wane away.
She clings to me with her tentacles
and begs me with grace.
But this new me doesn't have the energy or space.
To hold onto the past or give a voice to a variation.
That existed in a different world,
now just somewhere in my imagination.

I look into her frightened eyes,
just one last pitiful look.
It's time to leave her in the world of stories
because I am writing a brand new book.

Epilogue

Weeds (Reprise)

You will find me in the garden. Growing stronger each day. Emerald leaves sparkling like happy tears in the citrus sun. Dreams fluttering around my eyes like fairy wings and I can almost reach them. I don't have to wish to be a sunflower. I know I am the brightest sunflower with a buttercup smile, canary wings fluttering beside me, as I soar into the azure wilderness of possibility. You will find me in the garden. Growing stronger each day. No longer seeking an escape. Enamoured with life again. I am no longer a willow tree in a lonely meadow. I am surrounded by strong roots tangled with mine. I have so many souls that love me. The blessings kiss my eyes when I open them each morning. I still see shooting stars, but now I do not wish for change. I am praying for things to stay the same. For this blossom in my heart to stay on fire. For these healing brushstrokes to become bolder across my canvas. For me to find joy in wine and solace in self-love, to pick new colours to dye my hair, draw hearts around my scars and kiss them with gratitude and acceptance. For me to soak in every second and adore this new version of me. You will find me in the garden. Getting stronger every day. The flickering amber that survived is now expanding and learning to thrive. Yellow is my colour after all. The darkness can try and fight me. But I am supercharged with angel spirit. Nothing will stop me now from achieving greatness. The only voice I hear now is my own. The clarity I have been waiting to find for so many years is finally here. Endings birth new beginnings. My destiny is flowering and the bees are waiting to witness it all. The rise after the fall. Canary wings gaining their full strength. I close my eyes. I smile and I know it wasn't about being worthy. I was always a sunflower with canary wings. I just forgot that I knew how to fly.

Acknowledgments

To the man who broke my heart, thank you for setting me free.

To the men who were drops of ink in my story, thank you for the lessons.

To the man who is currently the caretaker of my heart, thank you for helping me on my healing journey and allowing me to believe in love again.

To all the friends in my life, thank you for your presence, your words and your light. You have gifted me the courage to be the best version of myself.

To my family for their support and understanding as I navigated through a challenging phase of my life.

To the person holding this book in their hands, thank you for giving my words a home. I hope these poems have opened your heart and given you the strength to believe that love conquers all.

Just remember, that no matter whom you give your heart to. Know that the one true love that will always last, is the love you have for yourself.

About the Author

Emma-Jane Barlow (known as EJ) is a northern poet, author, content creator, songwriter, singer and creative. She has been writing poetry since the age of seven and finds comfort in writing about her life experiences. From living life through an autistic lens to the highs and lows of love, loss and everything in between.

She has performed her poetry live at several events including C Arts Festival, Mic at the Mill, Natter, Salford Arts Theatre, Bask and Switchblade. She has also been featured in multiple anthologies including Chapters of Venus and Ink Gladiator Press. She has been featured in Salford Now newspaper and has been featured live twice on BBC Radio Manchester.

EJ shares her artistic journey on her Instagram page @emmajanepoetry and is also the founder of the successful collaborative poetry project First Line Poets @firstlinepoets.

In 2020, she self-published her debut book Darkness & Light, which became a multiple bestseller on Amazon, including the top 20 bestselling books for British poetry. She released her first edition of Sins & Sunflowers in 2022. She is also the editor of The First Line Poets Anthology.

She is working on her third poetry book and is exploring other creative projects to find new ways to express her love of storytelling.

DID3658272
L - #0255 - 140823 - C0 - 210/148/7 - PB - DID3658272